break dancing

LET'S DANCE

Aaron Carr

LET'S READ

AV²
BY WEIGL™
ADDED VALUE • AUDIO VISUAL

Go to **www.av2books.com**, and enter this book's unique code.

BOOK CODE

P786719

AV² by Weigl brings you media enhanced books that support active learning.

AV² provides enriched content that supplements and complements this book. Weigl's AV² books strive to create inspired learning and engage young minds in a total learning experience.

Your AV² Media Enhanced books come alive with...

Audio
Listen to sections of the book read aloud.

Key Words
Study vocabulary, and complete a matching word activity.

Video
Watch informative video clips.

Quizzes
Test your knowledge.

Embedded Weblinks
Gain additional information for research.

Slide Show
View images and captions, and prepare a presentation.

Try This!
Complete activities and hands-on experiments.

... and much, much more!

Published by AV² by Weigl
350 5th Avenue, 59th Floor
New York, NY 10118

Website: www.av2books.com   www.weigl.com

Library of Congress Control Number: 2013941097
ISBN 978-1-48961-750-7 (hardcover)
ISBN 978-1-48961-751-4 (softcover)

Printed in the United States of America in North Mankato, Minnesota
1 2 3 4 5 6 7 8 9 0 17 16 15 14 13

052013
WEP220513

Project Coordinator: Jason McClure   Designer: Mandy Christiansen

Weigl acknowledges Alamy and Getty Images as the primary image suppliers for this title.

LET'S DANCE

break dancing

CONTENTS

I love break dancing.
I am going to dance today.

4

Break dancers
often have
dance battles.

5

I dress for my break dancing class. I wear jeans and a T-shirt.

Dance Clothes

Break dancers often wear baggy clothes.

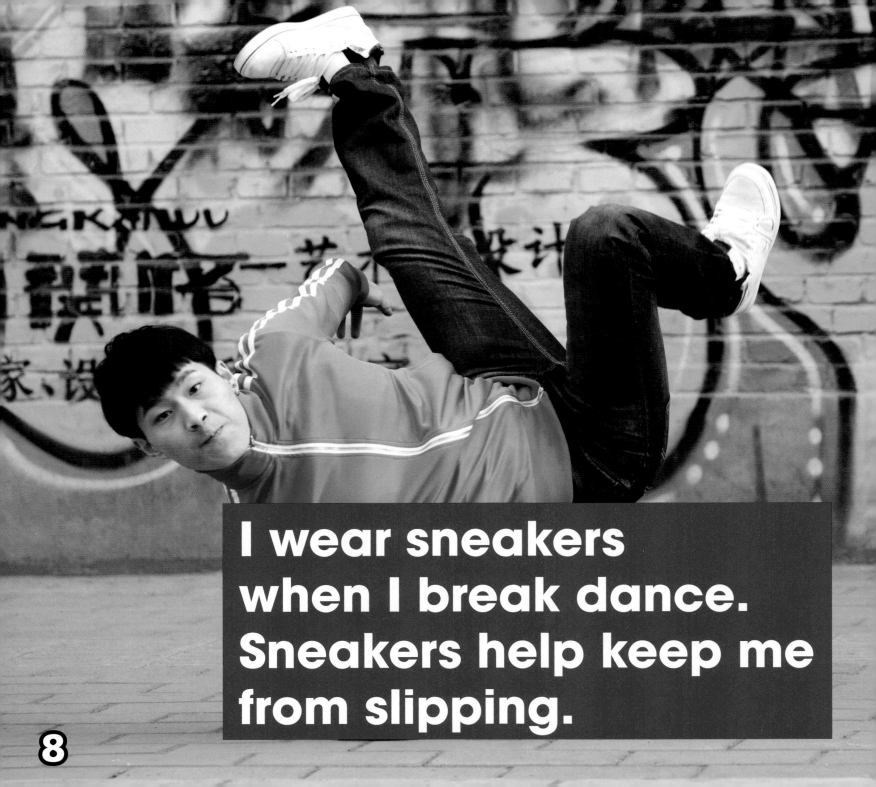

I wear sneakers when I break dance. Sneakers help keep me from slipping.

Dance Style

Many break dancers also wear hats.

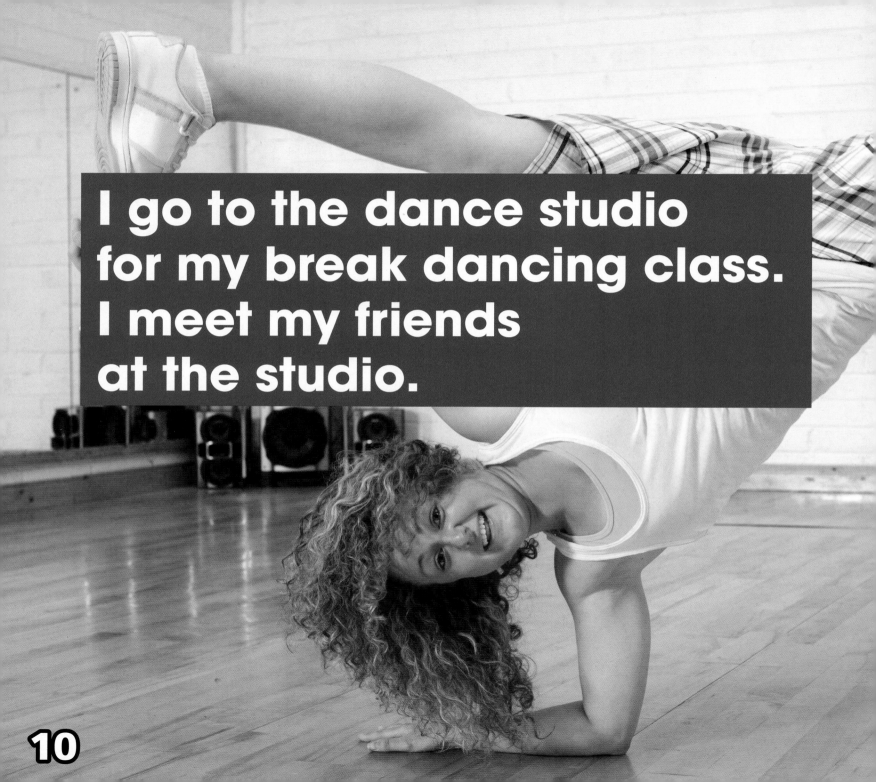

I go to the dance studio for my break dancing class. I meet my friends at the studio.

Break dancers sometimes dance outside.

I stretch to warm up before class. Stretching gets my body ready for break dancing.

Stretch it Out

Stretching helps dancers become more flexible.

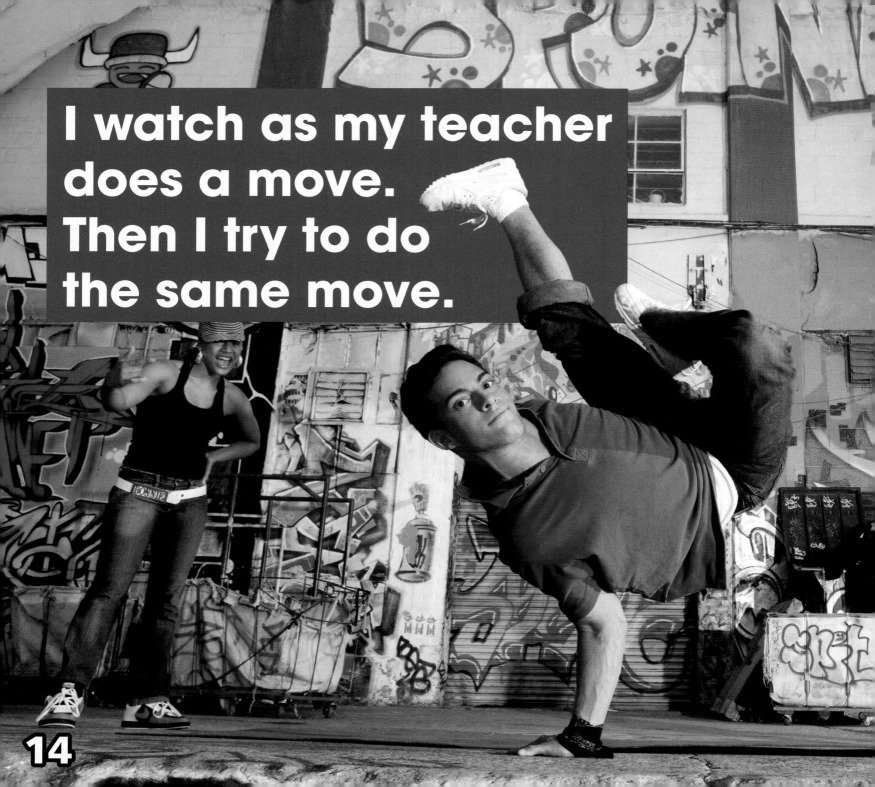

I watch as my teacher does a move. Then I try to do the same move.

14

Break dancers start by learning to toprock.

15

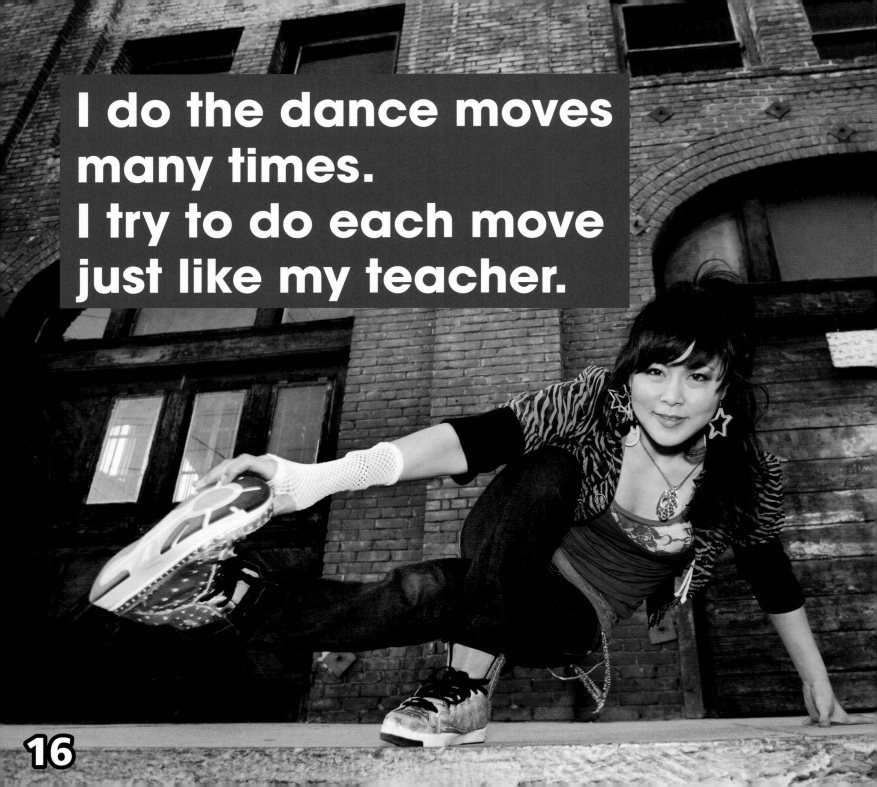

I do the dance moves many times.
I try to do each move just like my teacher.

16

Dance Work

It takes lots
of practice
to learn break
dancing moves.

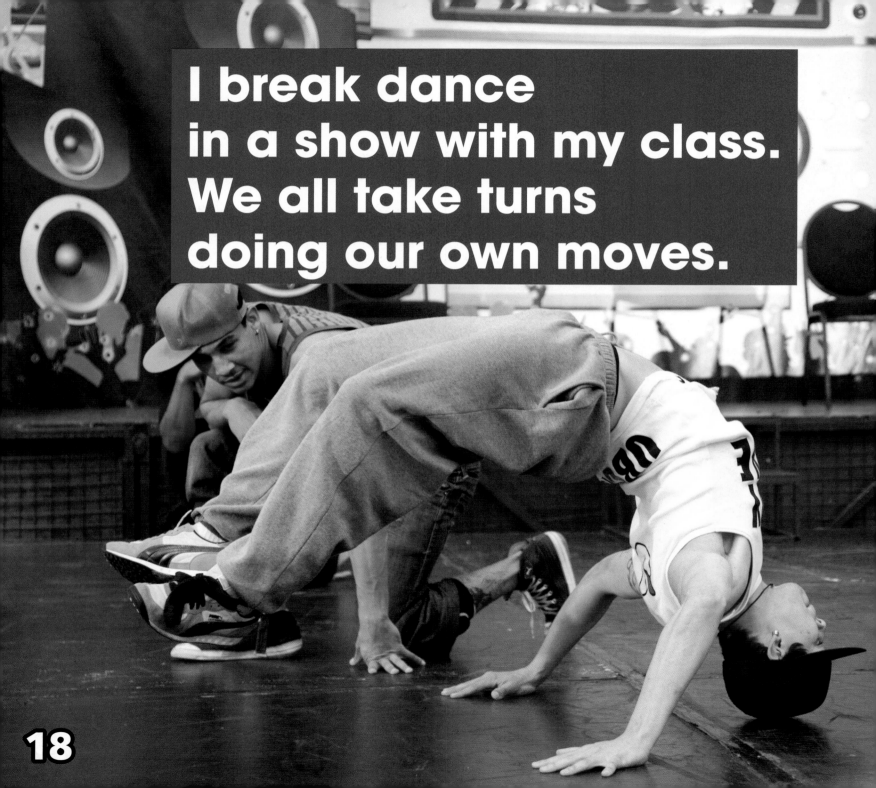

I break dance
in a show with my class.
We all take turns
doing our own moves.

Dance Groups

Break dancing groups are called crews.

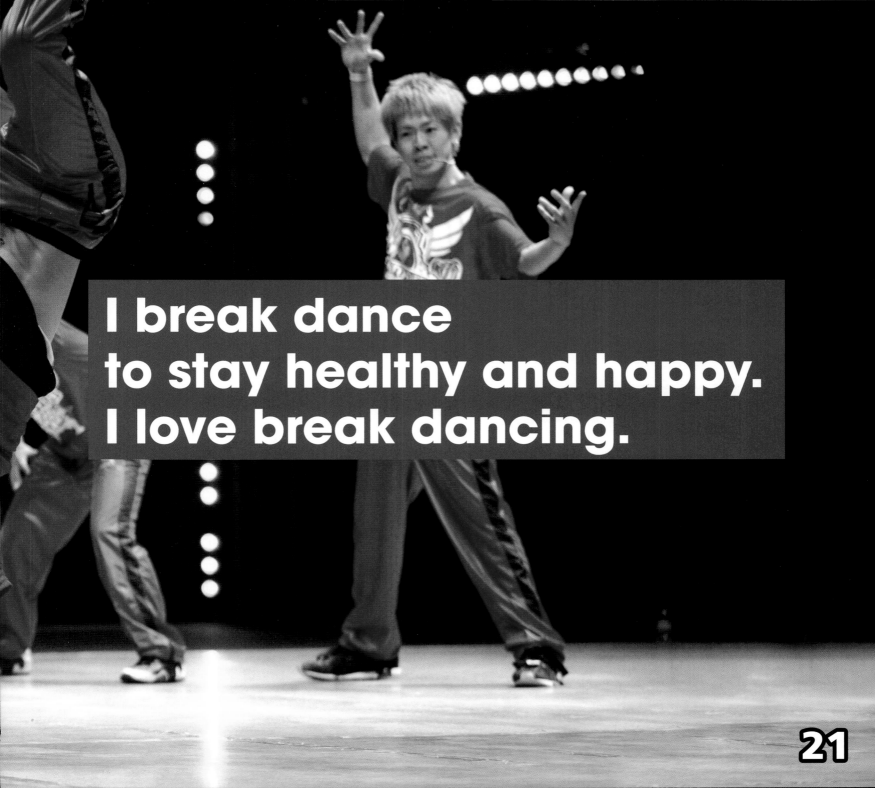

I break dance
to stay healthy and happy.
I love break dancing.

21

BREAK DANCING FACTS

These pages provide more detail about the interesting facts found in the book. They are intended to be used by adults as a learning support to help young readers round out their knowledge of each style of dance featured in the *Let's Dance* series.

Pages 4–5

Getting Ready Break dancing began as a style of street dancing in the 1970s. Often called breaking or B-boying, it features high-energy moves such as spins, jumps, and flips. Break dancers are called B-boys or B-girls. Break dancers often hold dance battles. These competitions put dancers against each other in a dance-off to see who has the best skills.

Pages 6–7

What I Wear There is no dress code for break dancing. Most B-boys and B-girls, however, wear baggy clothes. Jeans and T-shirts are common, as are shorts and track suits. Break dancing clothing should be comfortable and loose. This allows the dancers a wide range of motion through the legs, arms, and the upper body. Loose clothing is also an important part of B-boy culture.

Pages 8–9

What I Need Break dancers usually wear regular sneakers when breaking. Sneakers are comfortable and offer support for the feet and ankles. They also provide great traction on most surfaces. Sneakers are ideal for dancing on pavement or concrete, which are common surfaces used in breaking. Some dancers wear special sneakers with split soles for more flexibility in the feet.

Pages 10–11

Where I Dance Dance studios are open, large rooms. This gives dancers plenty of space to practice their moves. Studios often have sprung floors. Sprung floors are flexible. This lessens the impact dancers feel on their feet and legs when they perform jumps and other dance moves. At least one wall is covered in mirrors, allowing dancers to check their form.

Pages 12–13

Warming Up Stretching before and after dancing is very important. Injuries can happen if a dancer has not stretched properly. Break dancers do a variety of stretches for their legs and upper bodies. Breakers may use a barre to help them stretch. A barre is a horizontal rail that is often attached to the mirrored wall of the dance studio.

Pages 14–15

Learning the Moves Dance classes have one or more teachers who instruct students on proper dance forms. Teachers demonstrate moves to the students. Then, they help the students repeat the moves. All moves in breaking fall into one of four categories: toprock, downrock, power moves, and freezes. Beginners start with toprock, which are steps done in a standing position.

Pages 16–17

Practicing Learning to break dance requires a great deal of practice. Even the most basic moves take hours of practice to learn properly. As dancers move up through the dance school system, moves become more challenging and the amount of practice needed increases. For most dance schools, beginning dancers have one class each week. Older dancers may practice two or more times a week.

Pages 18–19

Show Time Most dance schools have one recital at Christmas and one in spring or summer. For a recital, students practice a set of dance moves called a routine. At the recital, they wear costumes and perform that routine to music. Family and friends come to watch and support the dancers. Wishing a dancer good luck before a performance is actually considered unlucky. Instead, people say "break a leg."

Pages 20–21

Staying Healthy Breaking is a great way to stay active and healthy. It promotes physical fitness and flexibility. Eating healthy foods is important for a dancer to get the greatest benefit from breaking. Dancers should eat foods such as fruits, vegetables, and whole grains. These foods will give the body the energy it needs to perform its best.

KEY WORDS

Research has shown that as much as 65 percent of all written material published in English is made up of 300 words. These 300 words cannot be taught using pictures or learned by sounding them out. They must be recognized by sight. This book contains 50 common sight words to help young readers improve their reading fluency and comprehension. This book also teaches young readers several important content words. These words are paired with pictures to aid in learning and improve understanding.

Page	Sight Words First Appearance	Page	Content Words First Appearance
4	am, I, to	4	break dancing
5	have, often	5	battles, fact, dancers
6	a, and, for, my	6	class, jeans, T-shirt
8	from, help, keep, me, when	7	clothes
9	also, many	8	sneakers
10	at, go, the	9	hats, style
11	move, sometimes	10	friends, studio
12	before, gets, up	12	body
13	it, more, out	14	teacher
14	as, do, does, same, then, try, watch	15	toprock
15	by	17	practice
16	each, just, like, times	18	turns
17	learn, of, takes	19	crews
18	all, in, our, own, show, with		
19	are, groups